Seasons of Life in Poetry

Jenie Fuerte Almalbis

Seasons of Life in Poetry

Seasons of Life in Poetry © 2022

Jenie Fuerte Almalbis

All rights reserved.

Presentation by *BookLeaf Publishing*

Web: www.bookleafpub.com

E-mail: info@bookleafpub.com

ISBN: 9789395756358

First edition 2022

Seasons of Life in Poetry

DEDICATION

To my Daddy, as promised, I will continue to make you proud.

Seasons of Life in Poetry

ACKNOWLEDGEMENT

Many thanks to my family who have been my source of strength and motivation all throughout the different seasons that I experienced in my life. Most especially to my mom and dad, the reason for my being.

To my Lola Tini, thank you so much for your love that has made me resilient all these years.

To my sisters Jelou and Coralynn, for always listening and encouraging me to never give up.

To Paul, for being a good friend, listener and constant support. For all the smart advice and encouragement, I am truly grateful.

To Ate Elna, I could never thank you enough for helping me to keep my sanity intact and push me to go further.

To friends who were constantly there regardless of my circumstances and distance. Thank you for the continuous support and love.

To each and everyone who have been a part of my journey and gave me inspiration.

Ultimately, to God almighty, my guiding light and everything.

Seasons of Life in Poetry

Seasons of Life in Poetry

PREFACE

In life, we experience different seasons. From when we were young, forging our dreams and how to achieve it and eventually living the dream and exploring places for more inspiration. To building relationships and falling in love and then getting our hearts broken or disappointed at times. To encounter the facets of life and learning how to tread and accept the truth about human existence. That loss is inevitable. That our time here on earth is not permanent. This poetry book speaks of the different seasons that I have experienced in my life as well as those people close to me that have shared their experiences and gave me inspiration. I wish that this book will give you some comfort and joy and lift you up as it touches your heart, especially on days when you feel like you are lonely and misunderstood. May it also allow you to see a different perspective in each season that we are in at the moment of our lives. It may seem easier said than done but always remember that there is someone out there who understands and feels what you are going through. There is someone out there who will be with you as you go through each season. There will be people around who will show genuine love and will listen even if you think that your voice is too small or that you don't matter. Because the truth is that you are loved and you matter. It may seem daunting on how to surpass each season, but never forget that there is always hope for as long as we have faith and believe that things will be okay.

Seasons of Life in Poetry

Seasons of Life in Poetry

I

BEHIND HER PEN

Some people ask why write?
Is it my way of respite?
Or just a form of escapism
So I can put my life back in rhythm

I write because I want to express
Those feelings that I try to suppress
So they can be released
And give myself some peace

I write so you may know
As it may somehow help us grow
To provide us clarity
For us to avoid disparity

I write hoping to reach your heart
Maybe you will understand
And you might extend your hand
And thus be able to restore our bond

It's not easy, contrary to what you see
How each word was written
As a part of me is ripping
But somehow leads toward healing

So I will keep on writing
Putting together those words and rhymes
Not only just to pass time
But most of all for it to motivate and inspire.

II

THE FILIPINA

She is strong and bold
And won't stop until she gets her gold
She is confidently beautiful and smart
Able to spread love with her big heart

They sometimes look down on her
But that won't stop her from getting better
She fights to the very end
Despite of all the criticisms people send

She will continue to remain resilient
Regardless of all the predicament
For her faith is unyielding
That's why her strength is everlasting

She will punch in every opportunity
Regardless of the difficulty
Working hard day and night
Giving her best and mightShe is a Filipina

And no matter which continent
She will raise her flag and stand tall
Regardless of how many times she falls.

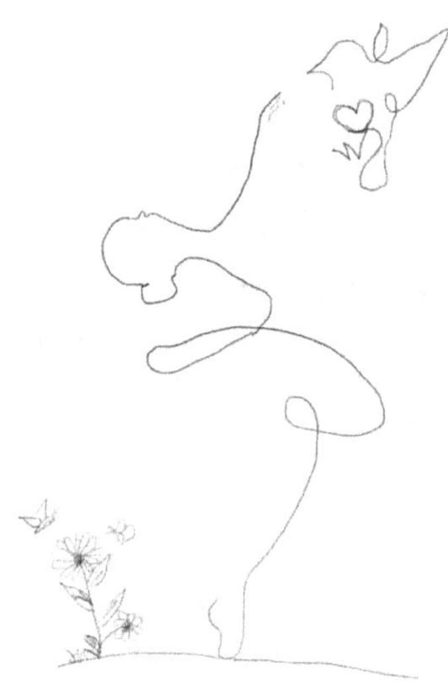

III

HIDDEN GLOW

In the vastness of the universe
She doesn't seem to notice
How much her beauty sparkles
In every direction and angles

She is so oblivious
With her light that is contagious
She does things with so much humility
And that's what makes her so pretty

Truly a rare gem to find
A lady with a beautiful heart and mind
She does have her flaws
But that doesn't make her pause

She will stand up with conviction
Despite the contradiction
For her faith is unwavering
And that's what keeps her glowing

IV

SLUMBER

It's been awhile
Since her last smile
One that brightens up the room
And blows away all the gloom

She longs for that embrace
As warm as the sun rays
She got the chill breeze instead
As she tries to sleep in her bed

It was three in the morning
Tears just won't stop flowing
Begging and praying
For the pain to stop hurting

What else is there to do
She's done everything she could
She's burning like a firewood
Slowly disappearing for good

However, an angel came to visit
To extinguish the fire that's lit
To whisper in her ears
And give her strength to fight her fears

Suddenly there was a deafening silence
A light glowed with so much brilliance
Her heart beat faster as her body perspire
And there the miracle transpires

Perhaps one day pure bliss will find her
Where love and peace surrounds the air
Gently hugging her as she goes to slumber
And there ending the nightmare.

V

DREAM AWAY

I had a dream last night
It filled my heart with so much light
It was about me and you
And how we started something new

I can see myself smiling again
And you no longer carrying any burden
It was as if we both have forgotten
The story of our past that was written

As I awake from that slumber
I hope I could remember
That seemingly happy feeling
As it helps with my healing

I wish I can prolong that dream
As it shuts memories that makes me scream
But I know I need to wake up
So my life can once again start.

VI

JUST BELIEVE

Once upon a time she looked up into the sky
She wondered if she could ever soar high
Then one day she got told she's about to fly

Her prayers were answered
It took her by surprise that it was heard
As uncertainties came but now it's confirmed

The beginning of a new chapter
A life journeying to many adventures
And many memories to capture

It's scary to hop on a plane
And go to an uncharted terrain
With unfamiliar faces and name

But life will not wait for us forever
It's either now or never
Or otherwise you'd be left to wonder

So take courage and decide
For you never know when things will coincide
Just believe for everything will abide.

VII
PRETTY LITTLE GIRL

There was this pretty little girl

Who was so afraid to twirl

But then one day she decided to try

There was nothing to lose anyhow

Even if she doesn't have a clue

And uncertain of what to do

She still decided to push through

It's amazing to experience something new

We get to see life in different hues

And look at how it transpires in several views

And so the pretty little girl that came by

Was no longer afraid to fly

She was up in the sky

And was suddenly soaring so high.

VIII

PUSH

When you wake up each morning
And you don't seem like moving
Remember your reason for living
And don't forget that life is a blessing

Days will turn into years
And it maybe hard to dry those tears
Caused by so many fears
But do not let it stop your prayers

Just keep on going
Until the sun is setting
For the difficult days will only be fleeting
And the good days ahead are coming

IX

PURE LOVE

We all have our own love story
That will forever be etched in our memory
Some ended up in weddings
Whilst others have bittersweet endings

There's a love that's unrequited
Hoping one day it will be united
There's a love lost and found
Faith was all it took for it to resound

To love and be loved
Is one amazing experience to have
It can give you profound happiness
Removing all feelings of loneliness

But Love that is pure and genuine
Can only come from heaven

So never lose hope in prayer
Because God will answer and deliver.

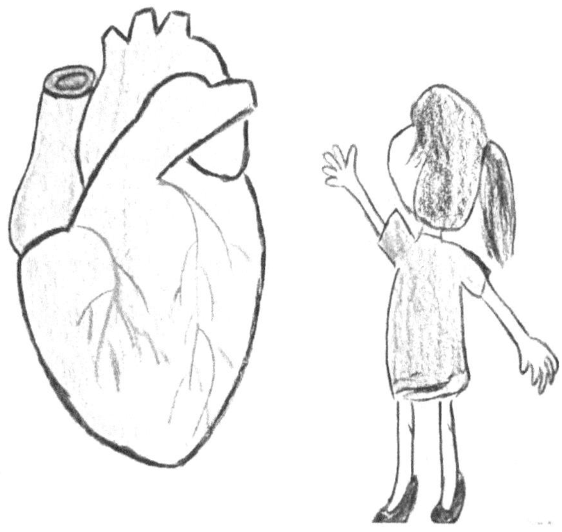

X

HEALING LOVE

Allow me to heal those wounds of the past that
still linger.
Let my love pulsate through your veins to
proliferate happiness in your system.
Hear my words and let it calm your soul.
Let every embrace leave memories in your ribs to
warm your heart.
The same way that you did to mine all this time.
For the love that you give is sublime.
Let this love we have invigorate the soul.
May it motivate and encourage,
To push us to become better
Not only for one another
But also for the people that love us so tender.
Ultimately, feel the force of my prayer and let it
nourish your spirit.
For I am most certain that what we have is
worth it.

XI

MOONLIGHT

I decided to take a stroll last night
Then I saw the moon just half in sight
He was hiding behind the clouds
I don't know if it was because my thoughts were
so loud
I wanted to ask him questions
That actually I later on realized were disguised
as lessons
Sometimes it's hard to understand why this has
to be
But then maybe there are moments when
understanding isn't the key
And just simply keeping your faith
For what the future awaits
Is everything that has to be.

XII

FLY ME TO THE MOON AND STARS

I once asked the moon and the stars

To grant my wish and heart's desire

That as I walk on this sandy beach

May it stretch out it's light within my reach

So I may find the right way

In order to help things become okay

And let the waves wash away

All things that makes everything grey

That in each sunrise of everyday

There'll be lots of hope to stay

More bliss and time to play

Under the warmth of the sun rays

Until it sets at the end of the day

So the moon and stars can again display

It's guiding light in the calm dark sky

Where our hopes and dreams soar high

XIII
WINTER SUN

As I awake on a winter morning,

It was cold, dark and freezing.

No light seen shining by the windowsill

What is this again I'm feeling?

Sadness suddenly starts to fill,

Mustering all hope and faith to stay still

My whole body shivers

What must I do to stop this quiver?

When anxiety comes to settle

It's very hard to stay level

So come and hurry now Mr. Sun

Your warmth can make it all gone.

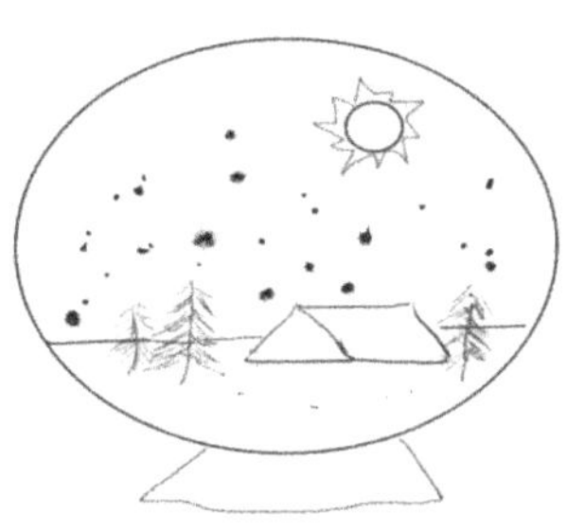

XIV

IT WILL BE OK

Hey, I know it's difficult again
And everything seems uncertain
But I hope you don't give up yet
Something amazing is set
That time will come soon
Everything will be revealed and known
You will see the reason behind the breaking
And appreciate all the blessings
Beyond all the hurting and crying
Comes your strength to rising and soaring
So get up and start moving
Begin your smooth sailing
And without you knowing
You are already up in the clouds and flying
Ready for new adventures and exploring.
For one small step means everything

XV

ABOVE WATER

One day you'll reach the surface.
One day your eyes will surely be amaze
For how beautiful life truly is
With all the wonders that bring pure bliss.
After you have reached rock bottom
And the emotions were so hard to fathom
Just hold on to your faith
Because it will help you to liberate
Unwanted thoughts and circumstances
That hinders you taking second chances.
Thus never lose hope and continue to trust
For you will make it at long last.

XVI

THE NORTHERN LIGHTS

Aurora Borealis is her name

From the sun flares is where she came

These silky spectres appear on a dark sky

So you better look up high

For she is a phenomena

Thus you should prepare your camera

Swaying silently or doing a waltz wistfully

Emitting various colours so brightly

Commonly looks like sheets of green.

Red, pink and purple are also often seen.

She brilliantly displays dynamic patterns

Appears as spirals, rays or curtains

Covering the earth's sky

Do you ever wonder how and why?

Caused by solar wind disturbances in the

magnetosphere

Altering trajectories of electrons and protons
in the atmosphere
How lovely is this lady
In the Arctic circle is where you have to be
To see and experience her magically
And appreciate her stunning beauty.
So if you ever want to find me
Remember that northern light lady
Glowing in the sky so magnificently
Like the love that I spread so genuinely
And that is why I am Legendary.

XVII

BLUE HOUR

Suddenly there was this dark cloud

Pouring memories that were so loud.

Then I remember it was that same day

When you decided to go away

Tears fall down in my eyes

Unable to accept your lies

For deep in my heart it knows

One day your true feelings will show

XVIII

HOPE SPRINGS ETERNAL

Finally, it's spring!

I look forward to what it will bring

This is the season where flowers bloom

Putting colours amidst the gloom

After a long slumber

From that cold and dark winter

On a bed of green grass

The daffodils are sprouting bright

Under this beautiful sunlight

One can only hope and pray

That spring will bring more beautiful days

And enjoy the warmth of the sun rays

This is also the perfect moment to achieve

All of our dreams and wishes if we just
believe.

For nothing is impossible

If we take a leap of Faith to make it feasible

Hope Springs eternal
And Love will be omnipresent for it is
essential.

XIX

PINK MUHLY

Have you ever seen such a land
Filled with cotton candy all around
They look so Pink and fluffy
How marvellous is this land of Muhly

Once I was traversing a field of wheat
Trying to find where we'll meet
But this is where I was brought by my feet
So I can breathe and sit

Everywhere around feels like a fairytale
It such a perfect place for me to tell
Of how much I truly fell
I could only wish it all went well

And as I lay on this lovely field of Pink
I could not help but wonder and think
Will I ever find my way back
And put my heart on the right track.

XX

A FRESH START

I lie awake in middle of the darkness
Awaiting for my sight back to be harness
Hiding away whilst hoping for nothing
And still insanely choosing him amidst the
hurting.
Never knowing if someone will arrive
Thus I just keep praying to keep me alive
You're buried deep inside me
But the truth I must accept and see
Why can't things be less complicated?
Why can't we just stop the hatred?
Until when will I wait for light to come?
For I so long to see the shining sun.

XXI

PAIN PAIN GO AWAY

Sometimes we wonder how to start
After we have fallen apart
Sometimes the path looks dark
And we just don't see any spark

We asked again and again
How do we end this pain?
Does it ever go away?
Or it is here forever to stay.

Days turn to a year
Yet the pain is still here
But somehow the gravity is not the same
As we learn to live with it since it came

Maybe one day it will just fade
Especially with the strength that was made
As we battle through our way
Towards healing that will surely come one day.

XXII

THE TRUTH ABOUT PAIN

I think it is such a cliché.

Especially when people say,

Time heals all wounds.

But what if it was so profound?

Is there really healing?

From all the pain that we're experiencing

Do we really fully recover?

Or just have days that we are sober.

The truth is the pain never goes away

It is there to stay

To probably be a reminder

That for as long as life isn't over

We need to keep on going

Despite of the aches we're feeling

For it has left us a valuable lesson

And protect us for whatever reason

We may never fully heal
From all the pain we feel
Perhaps of how special the reason was
Life may then look unrelenting but it'll pass
There will be days when it'll come in waves
But have faith in love that'll come to save
For better days will be around the corner
The hurt and suffering won't last forever.

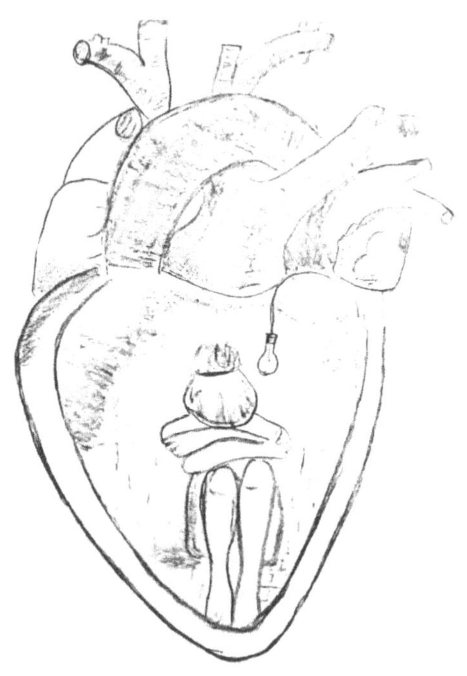

XXIII

HELLO JULY

It's amazing how the months have gone by
I can't believe it's already July
Half of the year have passed
With a blink of an eye all was cast
It has been filled with so much blessing
Mostly things I have been praying
Looking back right now
I still don't know how
When everything seemed impossible
I'm just glad I survived the obstacle
So I wont stop aiming high
I will surely soar fly in July.

XXIV
FINDING JOY

They say only time can predict
When your heart will again beat
After it has been torn into pieces
And brought you down to your knees
But how long does one endure the pain
For oneself to regain
To have that genuine smile and happiness
Even with just the simplest of things
Perhaps one needs to look back
In order to be on the right track
Muster all courage to feel the hurt
Dive and swim through all the emotions
To find clarity and understanding
So it can lead us to acceptance
Transforming those days of mournings
To a beautiful and better mornings.

XXV
YOU ARE LOVED

You are worth so much more than the
ordinary if only you could see.
You relentlessly chase your dreams and goals
turning them to reality
You have a mind that is so great and a heart
that ignites passion for love and kindness.
Your faith is bigger than your fears that
holds you together when things get tough
Brave soul, In His own way and time
everything will be alright again.
Remember, you've got this! Keep that focus.
You are loved.

XXVI

NEVER GIVE UP

Was there a time in your life
When nothing seems to feel right?
When darkness is all there is in sight
That you no longer have a strength to fight

After that very thing which kept you alive
Suddenly vanishes into thin air
And left you in despair
How can life be so unfair?

Was there a moment that you just wanted to
give up?
For all you want is the pain to stop
But it just kept on throbbing nonstop
That your body will just drop
How long will it be until this cycle of torment is
over?
Does one actually really recover?
But we need to trust the process

Even if it's slow there will be progress

Perhaps one day there'll be no more dark clouds
And probably love can thrive
For it heals all wounds
Regardless of how you got injured

For that light you carry can eliminate
Everything that makes you hate
And your path can illuminate
So the journey will become straight.

XXVII
BEFORE THE BOUGH BREAKS

I was sitting on a treetop

When suddenly a harsh wind blew

And as I was holding on

That is when I knew

It could be my last

As I have no more spells to cast

I will let go what's in my mind and speak

Before this bough breaks

Whether or not you will understand

I'd still take courage and hope you hold my
hand

I know there is no guarantee

But I'd rather try than live in a fantasy

XXVIII

A SEASON OF LOVE

It was summer when we first met
Our eyes gazed into each other
After cupid's arrow was set

It was autumn when we both started to fall
Hearts beating faster than ever
That is how I would recall

It was winter when we made lots of memories
Going on to different adventures together
Amazing journeys that we'll remember

It was spring when our feelings bloomed
Leading us both to go further
As we try to decipher our future

It was another fine day in summer
When suddenly everything became darker
And the sun never again shined brighter

Leaves starts to fall again
Perhaps it's time to begin
And let that beautiful life reign.

XXIX
MIRROR MIRROR

What do you see in the mirror?
Is it still terror?
I hope you are able to see
How the world appreciates your beauty

Those fine lines on your forehead
Those scars left when you tread
All challenges that life presented
Sleepless nights and crying in your bed

Remember you are beyond those marks
For your uniqueness brings joy and sparks
That even in the darkness
You can still bring happiness

What do you see in the mirror?
Is it still terror?
Or a flower blooming beyond the adversity
That has finally found tranquility.

XXX

AUGUST RUSH

What is your fondest memory of August?
Is it something you can treasure the most?
Like one of those that changes you
Even if it has made you feel blue

Mine was an answered prayer
Where the waiting felt like forever
But it gave me happiness I never knew
And had my world a different hue

It began with a smile and hello
Unexpected exchange of messages followed
Reluctant at first to respond
That is how we started our bond

Without any pressure
We both created a rhythm together

And like a classic love song
Thoughtfully I did hoped we can prolong

But you had a fickle heart
And that's why we fell apart
If only I knew perhaps I would have spared
That part of me that will be impaired

Years were ebbing away
And it's August again today
I can't help but reminisce
Perhaps there's something that I just miss

XXXI

THE ROAD

Life often leads us to different directions
Whilst some paths offer us protections
Others point us to several diversions
To introduce new perceptions

Oftentimes we go through transgressions
That sometimes bring us to depression
And people have these misconceptions Thus
most hide to limit giving explanations

But I think it will never disappear
All sad memories even if it's been years
For they are not only just reminders
But also lessons beyond the disasters

So when we're stuck on a crossroad
Let not these experiences put us on hold
Find a safe haven to sojourn
Until everything is again back in motion.

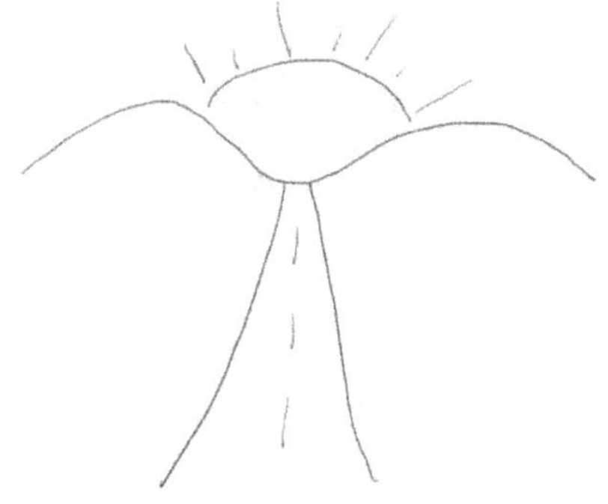

XXXII
WHEN AUTUMN MEETS WINTER

She was Autumn

Emulating resilience

Despite everything around losing its existence

She continues to bloom under the gloom

He was Winter

His heart was cold as ice

And brings darkness to the skies

But there's goodness if you look deep into his eyes

So when Autumn and Winter met

A moment of something beautiful was set

But autumn had to let winter reign

Even if it will cause pain

For the winter chill will pass
So she believed and took on those chances
For one day that frozen heart will melt
Then hope and love will be deeply felt.

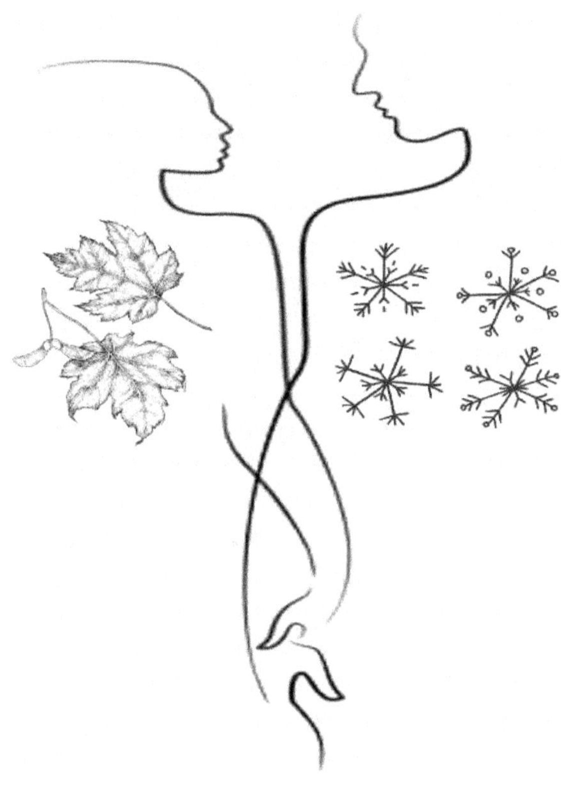

XXXIII

FALLING FOR YOU IN AUTUMN

From that moment at the corridor

On the month of October

When everything was losing life

You came along and revived my heart

With your every glance

My knees wobble that I lose my stance

And when you started talking

I find myself suddenly falling

I built more barrier

But you always seem to make it weaker

I tried to wear the cloak of invisibility

Your eyes though still see me

If I choose to reveal

Exactly how I feel

Are you gonna be different

Or will you choose to remain ambivalent

Then one day everything was clear
It's like you blown it on the atmosphere
The you and me will be a never
But I will cherish our time together.

XXXIV

AUTUMN IN MY HEART

How can you not fall?

On nature's creation that is so beautiful.

Notice the leaves on the tree

Transforming into gold is such a marvel to

see.

And even in the rain and dark

They still give this magnificent spark

Notice the crisp sound you hear

As you step on the leaves that are scatter

And the taste of pumpkin spice

On a chilly autumn night can surely entice

Nostalgic moments that make you smile

And warm your heart that will go for a mile

XXXV

SURVIVING THE FALL

The seasons have change
Yet everything still feels strange
There is this insurmountable pain
That is just hard to explain

Where do you get the sustenance?
How do you find the balance?
In order to surpass all these trials
That makes you leap a thousand miles

The days become shorter
And temperature gets colder
Signifying that here comes winter
Hopefully, these emotions are not forever.

For I believe Autumn is a time for healing
That even if everything around is dying

It is just a phase of transforming
And a preparation for the perfect moment of
rising.

XXXVI
THE END

Perhaps it really is sad to think of the end.

There won't be any chance to mend

For things that shouldn't have been

Or those that we should have forgiven

Perhaps it really is sad to think of the end.

For all thelove that we would've send

But now it's too late to make it shown

To the person who should have known

Perhaps it really is sad to think of the end

And we can no longer hide and pretend

All the emotions as it leaves us sadness

That makes it so hard to find happiness

But what if we shift our perspective

And allow ourselves to be introspective

We step back and start realizing
Why we are sad when something is ending

Then we will see the end is not really sad
For it was surely beautiful of what we had
Especially when it was happening
And it is just the beginning of an incredibly
beautiful thing.

XXXVII
ACCEPTANCE

When we are in a difficult situation
When there seem to have no explanation
On why certain things are happening
And we are just constantly battling
Over everything that life is throwing
Even if deep inside it is still baffling

When do we actually retreat?
Do we have to wait or just accept defeat?
Maybe it's okay to lose sometimes
Maybe it's actually pointing us to signs
Which will lead us to find clearance
Then eventually bring us to acceptance

XXXVIII
LIFE AS WE CALL IT

Not all of our plans in life will happen
There will be detours and delays more often
We will shed tears and our hearts soften
But surely will make our minds broaden.

Not everything we want will be given
And thus it will make us more driven
To achieve what we want
Even if life may well be daunt

Not all of the time we will have control
And so we get dismayed to reach our goal
So don't be bitter
Instead have faith for His plans are better

But in the end, even if things
Weren't what we were hoping
Even if it doesn't make sense right now at all
Surely one day, shower of blessings shall fall.

XXXIX

YOU WERE THERE

I have fallen

I've been broken

I was in shambles

I was in tears and aching

Not knowing when it'll stop hurting

But you were there

To pick me up when I'm down

To cheer me up when I'm about to frown

To encourage me when I'm losing hope

To help me find a way when I can't cope

You were there

To celebrate my small wins and success

To witness my rising after falling

To support me when I was rebuilding

To hold my hand when I am sick and fighting

You were there

To give me counsel when I'm confused

After being disappointed and bruised
I feel so blessed and lucky
For you were there in my story.

XL

YOU ARE NOT ALONE

When the skies are grey
And it feels like it's gonna be a hard day
Just close your eyes
Listen to the beat of your heart
Feel the rising of your chest
And remember Him in whom we can find rest
It may be hard to believe
Especially when we can't instantly achieve
That peace and comfort we ask and seek
But if we just remain meek
Surely we will find clarity
In our hearts and mind serenity
For He is our Lord almighty
And will always hold our hands tightly
So don't despair
Someone is with you to help repair
All the damage parts
And find a way again to start

XLI
FORGET ME NOT

When the sun rises and I am no longer there
to see,
Just know that my Father has called me.
When the flowers bloom in spring,
And the birds start to sing,
Just remember the joy I used to bring
Especially when I make those humming.

Perhaps tears will flow in your eyes,
But don't worry it's just a temporary goodbye.
No more pain and suffering
And there ending the hurting.
Just remember the wonderful memories we
made,
Whenever sadness visits so it'll fade.

I know someday we will meet again
Surely, it will be beautiful as it is in heaven

Where time is eternity
And a place where there is peace and
serenity.
There'll be days that you will feel sombre
But that feeling is evanescent and you will
recover

I am sorry I had to go away
I wish that I had more time to stay.
Never forget the love we shared.
And know that I sincerely cared.
I pray you find true happiness under the sun,
Even after I am gone.